T5-AQR-335

SOAR!

Effective Leadership Lessons

Effective Leadership Vol. 3

By
Marc Royer Ph.D.

SOAR!
Effective Leadership Lessons
Effective Leadership Vol. 3

Copyright 2005
Marc D. Royer
All Rights Reserved

Scripture quotations are taken from the New King James Version Copyright 1979, 1980, 1982, Thomas Nelson Inc. Used by Permission.

All rights reserved. No part of this book may be reproduced in any form, except for the inclusion of brief quotations in review or article, without the written permission from the author or publisher.

Published by:
The Christian Resource Group
717 Bainbridge Place
Goshen, IN 46526
(574) 533-5133
www.tcrg.org

ISBN 0-9705958-5-9
Library of Congress Control Number: 2004097547

Printed in the United States by Morris Publishing
3212 East Highway 30
Kearney, NE 68847
1-800-650-7888

OTHER BOOKS BY DR. MARC ROYER

Secrets: Exposing, Resolving & Overcoming the Secrets We Carry with Us
Handling Death Dying and Grief
Rejection: Turning Your Lemons into Lemonade
Happiness in 30 Days or Less
Financial Freedom Starting Today
Practical Patience
The Development Manual Series
Volume I: A Study in the Old Testament
Volume II: A Study in the New Testament
A Study in the Life of David
A Study in the Prophets
Hell No!
Square Peg, Round Hole
Hocus Focus
The Spiritual Warfare Manual
Go Hard or Go Home
Removing the Obstacles to Effective Leadership Vol. 1
Instructions in Opposition Vol. 2

Write:
The Christian Resource Group
717 Bainbridge Place
Goshen, IN 46526

Or visit our web site at www.tcrg.org
Request These Titles from Your Local Bookstore

TABLE OF CONTENTS

Introduction   **5**

1:    **Remember Where You Come from So You Will Recognize Where You Are Going**   **8**

2:    **Confess Your Sense of Destiny Every Day**   **20**

3:    **If You Aren't Seeing the Results You Want—You Are Just Looking for the Wrong Things**   **29**

4:    **Protect Your Own Motives**   **39**

5:    **Build Low-Maintenance Relationships**   **47**

6:    **Fortitude**   **62**

7:    **Take the High Road**   **72**

8:    **Go All the Way—Forget "Meet Me Half Way"**   **82**

9:    **Stay Up to Date**   **92**

10:    **Build Up**   **101**

11:    **Responsibilities of Leadership**   **112**

12:    **There Is Always Something to Learn**   **121**

13:    **You Don't Have to Get Nervous**   **128**

14:    **Work Hard and Only Work with Those Willing to Work Hard**   **137**

INTRODUCTION

The Apostle Paul selected Thessalonica as a strategic center to start a church. Located on the Egnatian Road, Thessalonica was at the center of the link between the East and the West. It was a thriving place of culture and commerce. A famous harbor in close proximity made the whole area important to Hellenistic culture, Roman government and Christian missionary strategy.

Paul had pattern for starting churches that he used as a template wherever he went. In Thessalonica his pattern was met with considerable converts from heathenism. So successful was he that a great amount of envy developed from opposition, (Acts 17:10) forcing Paul and Silas to leave the city by night.

They left behind a strong, growing church (1 Thessalonians 1).

After leaving Thessalonica, Paul went on to Berea to start another church. Word soon came that his new church was under severe persecution. He sent Timothy back to Thessalonica to help them and went on to Corinth to wait for news.

Sometime later, Timothy and Silas joined him (Acts 18:5) and brought the news about Thessalonica that the Apostle Paul was waiting for. The good report about the success of the church caused the exhausted Apostle to rejoice. It was with immense relief and personal affection that he wrote his first letter to the Thessalonians.

The success of this strategic missionary point was tempered by the problems they had at the leadership level of the church. Opposers of this ministry viciously slandered the Apostle Paul and others who led the church. Paul wrote them about spiritual vitality and growth. He challenged their moral laxness and slander.

Silas and Timothy, along with Paul, were most likely in Corinth when Paul wrote the second letter (2 Thessalonians 1:1). A comparison between the two letters indicates the second l etter w as w ritten close t o t he t ime h e w rote t he first (likely 3 weeks apart).

> # MORAL LAXNESS AND SLANDER WERE PROBLEMS IN FACE OF ALL THE SUCCESS.

The first letter had its proper effect upon those involved (2 Thessalonians 1:3 & 3:1-3). There were various problems concerning t eachings i n t he n ew c hurch, b ut t he p roblem t he Apostle Paul was dealing with in the second letter was the discipline of disorderly persons.

Paul writes to correct matters but also tries to encourage the persecuted and fainthearted.

The two letters to the Thessalonians opens up the heart of the Apostle Paul in a way the letters to Timothy or Titus don't. The church itself is opened up as well. We see the hopes, fellowship, discipline, and standards all laying out before us.

It is through these circumstances that we see lessons on effective leadership.

The point is: regardless of your circumstances you can SOAR! Here is a brand new church established through the vision of the Apostle Paul. While setting up this church, he received a couple of generous gifts from the people of Philippi. He used these resources to help the new project succeed.

The success was great (isn't it always?). There is always a "but" when it comes to success. In this case, the "but" resulted in huge problems. So it goes—whenever you have great success, you are going to have great problems. The answer is in developing effective leadership to deal with the problems associated with any endeavor.

The lessons of effective leadership are developed as we go. We all learn on the job. That is what happened in Thessalonica—and that is what happens today!

THE LESSONS OF EFFECTIVE LEADERSHIP ARE "LEARN AS WE GO" — EFFECTIVE LEADERSHIP IS THE ULTIMATE ON THE JOB TRAINING!

---

1 Remember where you come from so you will recognize where you are going!

Paul, Silvanus, and Timothy,

To the church of the Thessalonians in God the Father and the Lord Jesus Christ: Grace to you and peace from God our Father and the Lord Jesus Christ.

[2]We give thanks to God always for you all, making mention of you in our prayers, [3]remembering without ceasing your work of faith, labor of love, and patience of hope in our Lord Jesus Christ in the sight of our God and Father—1:1-3

Life is a continual educational process. **Effective leadership is that—plus some!**

Effective leaders always remember where they came from. Remembering this provides an opportunity to reflect on how far you have come. In the midst of this kind of thought process, we are able to get our brains around the possibilities of the future: **"If I have come this far, what are the limits to the future?"** There are no limits to the future! But then, there never were in the first place—you arrived at this conclusion by remembering where you came from.

Remembering where you came from has been a powerful process all through history. In the Bible, the Hebrews were constantly building monuments to memorialize the lessons they were learning about God's provision. **It is important for leaders to do the same.**

It might be difficult to teach yourself to remember where you came from "out of the blue" without some kind of application.

The "remember where you came from" thought process is created by applying several component parts of the process. Perfection is not necessary—this thought process is not difficult to develop. Simply work at one or two at a time and the others will fall into place as needed.

1. LOOK AT THE TRACK RECORD—HISTORY IS THE BEST INDICATION OF FUTURE PERFORMANCE—(EVEN YOUR OWN TRACK RECORD)!

This concept works at two different levels. If a leader will execute this concept at both levels, there will be a remarkable effectiveness when the leader needs to help with inserting wisdom into any situation.

The first level is when you need an indication as to what a person's future performance will be.

Before putting a person to work—paid or volunteer—check them out with others. A resume will often indicate who the person you are looking at has asked to provide references or to vouch on his or her behalf. Don't ever confine your research to just these people. Find out the impression of others about this person. The things you hear will indicate how this person will be thought of by others who work for you.

Listen to how the person you are interviewing talks. Are they negative about their last boss or last job? If they are, it will only be a matter of time before they are this way about you. It will be you they are talking about at their next interview. History is the best indication of the future. What they say about the last boss today, they will be saying about you tomorrow. (Unless you think you are so different as a leader that everyone loves you). If this is the case—**get over yourself!** The person you are interviewing is giving you every indication as to who they are. If you have a reservation about them in any way—don't put them to work.

The second level is when you are nervous about a situation you are facing. There are times when you have to talk to your own brain. You have to remind yourself that God has always seen you through.

What about this situation is so different that God won't help you this time?

There isn't anything in your answer that is even close to being valid—anything that comes to mind is simply a projection of your own guilt and insecurity. God's desire to help you in your past (and even more so in your future) transcends both guilt and insecurity.

If God has helped you before, He will help you again. Nothing could possibly happen to change this fact.

GOD IS GOING TO HELP YOU THIS TIME JUST LIKE HE HAS EVERY OTHER TIME!

The idea here is when you are looking at your own track record, you are looking at God's track record. He said He would never leave us and nothing has happened to change that promise.

Leadership can be a nerve racking experience. Add to it this different issues every leader brings to their leadership—the need to control; perfectionism; the obsession to fix it; and many others. It becomes hard for a leader to put aside all the issues to come back to the simple truth. **Regardless of me, (or my issues) God is going to make provisions for my success just like He always has.**

2. ALWAYS BE THANKFUL—EXPRESS IT THROUGH AFFIRMING OTHERS!

Thankfulness has a way to break through any attitude, either personal or corporate. It is contagious and positive. It helps a leader regain and maintain a better perspective in any situation.

The best expression for thankfulness is to be affirming toward the people around you.

An important target for a thankful spirit is for those people around you in your life.

It will be difficult to be thankful and express affirmation for others if all you see in others is their shortcomings. That is why it is so important to remember: **There is good in the worst of people and there is bad in the best—so—what you look for in people is what you are going to find.**

In this regard you will never find yourself being thankful in the face of the situations you encounter until you apply the same concept to your life: **There is good in the worst of situations and there is bad in the best of situations—so—what you look for is what you are going to find.**

Thankfulness is a choice! You can be thankful regardless of your circumstance—but only if you want to be.

Affirming and expressing appreciation to others is a choice as well. It requires a person to get past looking at themselves—and looking toward others.

Thankfulness does require a certain amount of boldness because people aren't used to someone affirming them. However, people are desperate to be affirmed. If you can just get started, you will learn quickly how thankfulness can change your own life—plus—how life-changing it is for others.

3. MAKE PRAYER THE MOST IMPORTANT MEETING OF YOUR DAY!

Prayer is more than just some mystical experience or something used as a challenge to make you feel guilty because you don't do enough of it. Prayer is a powerful connection that helps you remember where you came from so you will recognize where you are going.

- **Prayer makes you feel connected.** If you make it a first thing in the morning practice, you will feel connected all day long.

Leadership is a lonely experience. The more connected you feel, the stronger your leadership will be. The more connected you are, the clearer your communication will be.

- **Prayer renews your dependency on God.** We need this renewal every single day. If we forget, we end up feeling independent or self-gratified in what we are doing.

On the outside, it would seem like independence is what we are after—but an independent spirit does nothing but set a leader up for a terrible tumble.

Personal accountability is an important character trait. If a leader can't be accountable, he/she will never be effective in their leadership. The most accountable a person can be is when they are accountable to God—realizing He sees and knows everything there is to see and know.

Often people develop accountability groups to keep one another accountable morally and ethically in their lives. **The truth is if a person isn't accountable to God when no one is looking—that person won't be accountable.** Hence, prayer is the most important meeting of the day.

- **Prayer helps a person visualize their priorities.** Priorities can be so easily misplaced. The idea of spending time in prayer is the idea of revisiting priorities every single day.

- **Prayer gets things "out there" in the open.** Expressing something in prayer should get things up and out. This is important in formulating the direction of life. Holding something in doesn't do any good in leadership. Getting it out helps define an effective leader.

Every leader should set up a prayer time in their schedule. It should be considered the most important meeting of the day— and held up as such. This is personal meeting/prayer time. It shouldn't include other people. Even if people want to be included—don't do it—show them how to set up their own "most important meeting of the day" but have them do it on their own!

4. REMEMBER THE LESSONS YOU HAVE ALREADY LEARNED!

An often overlooked opportunity is a systematic analysis of what you have already learned. Everyone acknowledges what they have learned from time to time, but we often forget these lessons as time goes on.

It is important to imprint your mind with what you are learning so that you don't have to repeat your mistakes. That is why it is important to take time every single day to analyze what is being learned from what you are doing.

It is best done by setting up your own system. The more time you invest, the more honest you are, and the deeper you think—the more it will return to you. Ask yourself:

1. **What did I learn today from the duties I performed?**

2. **What am I the most proud of that I did today?**

3. **What am I the least happy with about myself today?**

4. **Could I have done something better?**

15

5. How would I d o t his n ext t ime t o improve o n h ow i t came out?

6. What did I learn from yesterday that helped me deal with my duties today?

7. What have I learned today that will help me with my duties tomorrow?

8. How can I apply all of this practically to my leadership? My life?

MAXIMIZING THE ANALYSIS

- *These questions could be typed out and spaces given to hand write a response.*

- *Block out 15 minutes toward the end of your day to do this exercise.*

- *Place your completed forms in a notebook by date.*

- *Review your forms once a month—20 of them—then use one more form to do an end of the month analysis.*

The goal is to learn as much as possible from the things you face from day to day. A leader finds that the days have a way of always running together. **If you don't make a concentrated effort to analyze your day, you will find them rolling on without the depth of knowledge you could really gain.**

5. LEARN FROM THE MISTAKES OF OTHERS!

There is much to be said about learning from the mistakes of others. No one has the time to make (and learn from) all the mistakes possible in a leadership endeavor. What we can do to maximize the possibilities is to make a conscious effort to learn from others.

This idea is not to be nit-picky or critical of others. The natural tendency of insecure people is to look down upon the efforts of others because it makes them feel bigger about themselves.

Learning from the mistakes of others requires two things:

1. **Make it your intention to let others be a resource to your learning experience in leadership.**

2. **Ask yourself: What can I do to avoid making the same mistake this person had made?**

These questions need to be personal issues that aren't discussed with others. If misused, they could appear very condescending. Yet, learning from the mistakes of others is essential in maximizing leadership development.

QUESTIONS FOR DISCUSSION

1. Explain how looking at a track record is important.

   _____

   _____

   _____

   _____

   _____

   _____

   _____

   _____

2. What is the key to being thankful when you don't feel like it?

   _____

   _____

   _____

   _____

   _____

   _____

   _____

   _____

3. Talk about the most important meeting of the day:

   _____

   _____

   _____

   _____

   _____

   _____

   _____

   _____

   _____

4. **What questions should you ask to help you learn from your mistakes?**

_____
_____
_____
_____
_____
_____
_____
_____
_____
_____
_____

5. **What further steps would you take to in learning from your mistakes?**

_____
_____
_____
_____
_____
_____
_____
_____
_____
_____
_____
_____
_____
_____
_____
_____

2 Confess your sense of destiny!

⁵**For our gospel did not come to you in word only, but also in power, and in the Holy Spirit and in much assurance, as you know what kind of men we were among you for your sake.** ⁶**And you became followers of us and of the Lord, having received the word in much a ffliction, with j oy o f t he H oly S pirit,** ⁷**so t hat you became examples to all in Macedonia and Achaia who believe.** ⁸**For from you the word of the Lord has sounded forth, not only in Macedonia and Achaia, but also in every place. Your faith toward God has gone out, so that we do not need to say anything.** ⁹**For they themselves declare concerning us what manner of entry we had to you, and how you turned to God from idols to serve the living and true God,** ¹⁰**and to wait for His Son from heaven, whom He raised from the dead,** *even* **Jesus who delivers us from the wrath to come. 1 Thessalonians 1:4-10**

The basic idea of "confession" is mostly for the person confessing—hearing yourself say it is vital in truly believing it. What is the "it?" "It" is whatever you need to have reinforcement on.

Every leader needs reinforcement once in a while. No one is exempt from needing validation for something said, something done, or something believed.

The number one need for every individual is the need to make a difference. This need is especially strong for the leader. Effective leaders have the passion at the deepest level to make a difference in the world around them. This passion creates both an energy level that drives a leader on and an energy drain if others don't catch the leader's passion. A mantra is needed for leaders to thrive in every circumstance—hence—the idea of **confessing your sense of destiny.**

This idea of confessing your sense of destiny needs to be broken down into smaller steps to build into a whole. The following six confessions is something that can be used all day long. If leaders are serious about keeping their energy level up and their passion to lead intact—then these six confessions will propel their quest to experience a sense of destiny in their leadership.

CONFESSION:

I AM CHOSEN BY GOD!

---

[4] **Knowing, beloved brethren, your election by God.**

Much of the discussion about this kind of concept ends up with people debating about whether some are chosen by God and others not chosen by God. When this discussion heats up, it misses the whole point behind it. **The idea of election is not about whether some people are chosen and others not—it is about how humankind was created and chosen by God.** It has to be discussed in light of eternity and God's plan—not me and my life!

During the heat of the day in the life of the leader—when the stress is the greatest—the confession needs to come up and out of the leader: **"I AM CHOSEN BY GOD."** This confession is a powerful reminder that no one is forgotten, no one is on their own, and no one has been left behind.

When a leader feels lonely, this confession needs to be the first thing that comes to mind. When a leader feels used, abused, or deceived—**"I AM CHOSEN BY GOD"** should quickly remedy the situation.

CONFESSION:

I AM A ROLE MODEL FOR OTHERS!

---

[5]For our gospel did not come to you in word only, but also in power, and in the Holy Spirit and in much assurance, as you know what kind of men we were among you for your sake.

When a person is exhausted, the last thing they care about is that they are a role model for others—an effective leader sees it differently. Effective leaders understand that one of the most important things about their leadership is not the words that come out of their mouth—but how they live their life!

What we do is what is modeled to others. It speaks much louder than words.

The fact that others are watching doesn't create tension in a leader—rather—it is seen as a challenge. A large part of leadership is the fact that others are watching. If they can't see you, you can't lead them.

The fact that a leader is a role model enhances the sense of destiny because the importance of what he/she does is magnified.

Whenever a leader is at a point of indecision—and especially indiscretion—he/she should confess: **"I AM A ROLE MODEL!"**

CONFESSION:

THERE ARE ALWAYS A FEW BUMPS AND BRUISES ALONG THE WAY!

---

⁶And you became followers of us and of the Lord, having received the word in much affliction, with joy of the Holy Spirit

Not that anyone needs a reminder but there are always going to be a few bumps and bruises along the way.

This confession should come from the leader several times through out the day—when things are going good and when things are going bad.

The reminder that there are always going to be a few bumps and bruises along the way is intended to create an alignment with the sense of divine destiny every leader needs to feel.

Just because things aren't going so good does not mean your sense of divine destiny is gone. In the same way, just because things are going good does not mean you have your sense of destiny more fine-tuned.

The fine-tuning in your sense of destiny comes from one thing: **confessing your sense of destiny throughout every day!**

CONFESSION:

I AM BUILDING ON SOMEONE ELSE'S BUILDING!

---

[7] So that you became examples to all in Macedonia and Achaia who believe. [8] For from you the word of the

Lord has sounded forth, not only in Macedonia and Achaia, but also in every place. Your faith toward God has gone out, so that we do not need to say anything.

Every leader must come to terms with the fact that they are making a contribution to help others—they are not changing "life as we know it on Planet Earth!"

A common mistake leaders make is how serious they take themselves. No one will be as intense about what you want, what you are doing, or what you want to accomplish as you are.

In the scope of how seriously we take ourselves, a leader often forgets that we are each making a contribution to the whole—what we are doing is not the most important thing.

It is most important that a leader not take him/herself too seriously.

One should always remember that everyone has different gifts and talents and each is making their contribution—our sense of destiny is based upon an abiding sense that the contribution being made is making a difference.

It is also important that every leader respect the contribution of their predecessor. The one coming before you is always an easy target because you will always find people willing to be negative about them. Don't find too much pleasure in it because you will eventually be a predecessor yourself.

You will reap what you sow in this regard. Be positive about all those who came before. Make your contribution with the feeling that your contribution has a destiny to it.

25

```
┌─────────────────────────────────────┐
│                                     │
│         CONFESSION:                 │
│                                     │
│                                     │
│      A SENSE OF DESTINY             │
│       MEANS I HAVE A                │
│      SENSE OF PURPOSE!              │
│                                     │
└─────────────────────────────────────┘
```

[9]For they themselves declare concerning us what manner of entry we had to you and how you turned to God from idols to serve the living and true God

Confessing a sense of purpose gives each day its own validation. It doesn't matter what area you lead—or what people you lead—often the responsibility of it is disorienting. This can happen to the most capable of leader. That is why declaring (confessing) a sense of purpose is so important.

"I have a sense of purpose" is more than just words—it is the essence of a divine destiny.

A sense of purpose and a sense of divine destiny drive each other. You can't have a divine destiny without a sense of purpose and you can't have a sense of purpose without a divine destiny!

```
┌─────────────────────────────────┐
│                                 │
│      CONFESSION:                │
│                                 │
│   I HAVE INNER PEACE            │
│   THAT IS DISPLAYED             │
│   THROUGH PATIENCE              │
│       IN MY LIFE!               │
│                                 │
└─────────────────────────────────┘
```

[10] And to wait for His Son from heaven, whom He raised from the dead, *even* Jesus who delivers us from the wrath to come.

Don't be scared—this confession is a mouthful for anyone! The importance of it is for every leader to hear themselves say that "I am patient." The footnote on this confession should be: "REPEAT THIS PHRASE AS OFTEN AS NECESSARY."

Patience is not natural (or even normal) for most leaders. If the concept can be adapted by way of thinking in terms of inner peace that gives me patience—then the whole idea can be brought down to size.

"I have an inner peace that provides me with patience in the face of anything" should be a real way to achieve a true patience in one's leadership.

QUESTIONS FOR DISCUSSION

Write down the six confessions and make personal application to each of them:

#1_____
_____
_____
_____

#2_____
_____
_____
_____

#3_____
_____
_____
_____

#4_____
_____
_____

#5_____
_____
_____

#6_____
_____
_____
_____
_____
_____
_____

3 If you aren't seeing the results you want—you are just looking for the wrong things!

2:1 For you yourselves know, brethren, that our coming to you was not in vain. ²But even after we had suffered before and were spitefully treated at Philippi, as you know, we were bold in our God to speak to you the gospel of God in much conflict. ³For our exhortation *did* not *come* from error or uncleanness, nor *was it* in deceit.⁴But as we have been approved by God to be entrusted with the gospel, even so we speak, not as pleasing men, but God who tests our hearts. ⁵For neither at any time did we use flattering words, as you know, nor a cloak for covetousness—God *is* witness. ⁶Nor did we seek glory from men, either from you or from others, when we might have made demands as apostles of Christ.

Rarely is a leader satisfied with how things are going. Generally, there is always something we could be doing better—or something could have gone better. Plus—leaders usually pour over records and statistics—so they become very important in tracking, accountability, and projection.

Because of how a leader is trained—and geared up for results—they usually spend quite a bit of their time analyzing why things are not happening the way they are supposed to—or how they want them to.

This part of the Apostle Paul's teaching is not about when you are getting the results you want—**it is for when y ou a ren't**

getting the results you want. It doesn't matter how good you are, there are always going to be those times when you are disappointed or frustrated by how things are turning out—that is when you apply this teaching to your life.

More than just "simple reminders", these ideas can get your mind back to the place it needs to be when things aren't going the way you want them to be.

If things are going well in your organization—**good for you!** If not, read on—but also remember where to turn to (chapter 3 of volume 3) when things aren't going as well. **Because no matter how good you think you are, there will always come the time when the results don't seem like enough for the effort you are putting in.**

NOTHING A LEADER DOES IS EVER "IN VAIN."

2:1 For you yourselves know, brethren, that our coming to you <u>was not in vain.</u>

When leaders get geared into the numerical result of their work, they end up forgetting that their contribution to life is larger than how the numbers reflect the importance of that result.

If the organization emphasizes the numbers, the message is sent that your worth to the organization is based upon the reflection of numerical reports, statistics, and results.

Most organizations make the numbers an important part of what they do. There is a certain amount of reality here. Organizations have to produce results to stay in business. What organizations forget, however, is everything we do in life is seasonal. There are going to be good times with great results—and—there are also going to be hard times with terrible results. There are going to be times where you don't have to work very hard to thrive. There are going to be times where everyone works their tail off and nothing happens.

Because of all this, every leader needs to realize that nothing you do is ever in vain. Everything done produces a result— even though you can't see the result being produced, it is still happening!

YOU CAN'T ALWAYS "FIX IT"—SO LEARN TO LIVE WITH CONFLICT.

2:2 But even after we had suffered before and were spitefully treated at Philippi, as you know, we were bold in our God to speak to you the gospel of God in much conflict.

The Apostle Paul shares that the conflict made them even bolder.

- **They suffered in their leadership but it made them bolder.**
- **They were treated spitefully but it made them bolder.**

How can a leader become bolder in their leadership when under conflict? Because effective leaders resolve that they don't have to "fix it" up. The leader is responsible to lead—not control the situation. The leader has to lead—not please people.

Further: If a leader doesn't experience conflict once in a while, nothing is really progressing. Progress means conflict will be present. There is no amount of public relations, smoothing things over, or people pleasing that will cause a leader to be able to "fix it" at times. An effective leader realizes some things can't be fixed—it only means you are progressing.

It can become a real frustrating point when you are not seeing the results you are looking for and the conflicts around you intensify. This usually happens in an organization when leaders realize they are not going in the direction they want to be headed in their calculations and reports. Blame is assessed, excuses presented, and all the time, the conflict level is rising.

It is during these tough times that a leader must realize that **I am seeing results—they are just not in the ways I usually see them.** Learning that you can't "fix it" is an important and powerful lesson for leaders. It sometimes takes several times through the cycle of results for those leaders to finally "get it" that they can't always "fix it."

LET YOUR OWN CLEAR CONSCIOUS BE ENOUGH "RESULTS" IN YOUR LIFE.

2:3 For our exhortation *did* not *come* from error or uncleanness, nor *was it* in deceit.

Living your life honestly and treating people fairly has a reward all its own—a clear conscience. This should be our foundational goal. Honesty and fairness should be supreme above all other things. You can be right or wrong—or—appear right or wrong, but if you lack honesty and fairness, you don't have anything in your life really worth having. Further, you can produce all the positive results your organization could ever want, but if you lack honesty and fairness, the results don't really matter.

A leader should embrace the idea of a clear conscience as greater than any kind of numerical result.

PLEASING GOD ALWAYS GIVES YOU A "RESULT"— PLEASING PEOPLE RARELY DOES.

2:4 But as we have been approved by God to be entrusted with the gospel, even so we speak, not as pleasing men, but God who tests our hearts.

Trying to gain the approval of people is an endless task because the criteria for approval are constantly changing. What pleases people one minute will turn them off the next.

The way we please God is by obeying His Word (which is set up for our lives). The way this works is for a person to take the Bible as substantive for one's life. It isn't just a bunch of stories, but also of principles for living and personal development.

Pleasing people never gives you the result you are looking for in the endeavor. The reason for this is it requires so much energy to please people that you never get back what you put into the situation.

If you are looking for the approval of your boss—the potential satisfaction will never meet the expectation. There is always disappointment if you do things for the boss. Raise the bar—reach higher—look to please God rather than humankind with your efforts. He is always pleased with you—and you can know that He is there through the inner peace you will gain as a result of seeking to please God rather than people.

SPEAK DIRECTLY AND HONESTLY—IT IS ITS OWN REWARD.

2:5 For neither at any time did we use flattering words, as you know, nor a cloak for covetousness—God *is* witness.

The Apostle Paul was always mentoring his young leaders to speak directly and honestly. He wanted them to be responsible for the words that came out of their mouths.

In the same way, we should be responsible for the words that come out of our mouths. Honesty and directness in what we say is much more important that the achievement of statistics in an organization.

Organizations often get themselves imperiled by regarding results of their leaders as greater than the directness and honesty in the communication of their leaders. If results are the driving force behind an organization, they will soon discover that they have been blind to things that matter more than numbers.

IF YOU DON'T EXPECT GETTING NOTICED, YOU WILL NEVER BE DISAPPOINTED.

2:6 Nor did we seek glory from men, either from you or from others, when we might have made demands as apostles of Christ.

When it comes to "results" of our leadership, it has to come down to this: **We can't stake the measure of our worth on the measure of our work.** If we do—we will always lose! There is no way to that a person can stay ahead of the pressure of numbers anyway—let alone if you tie your measure of self - worth to the reflection of your work.

Learn to utilize these verses from chapter 2 as a way to train yourself away from looking at only the organization's criteria of success!

QUESTIONS FOR DISCUSSION

1. **What are some of the reasons why a leader is often dependent upon their measurement of result?**

_____

_____

_____

_____

_____

_____

_____

_____

_____

_____

2. **How would you apply the idea that nothing you do is ever in vain to your leadership?**

_____

_____

_____

_____

_____

3. **Was there ever a time when you were successful by the standards of others, but that your conscience was not clear? Describe the situation.**

_____

_____

_____

_____

_____

4. Profile the difference between pleasing God and pleasing people as you see it.

_____
_____
_____
_____
_____
_____
_____
_____
_____

5. What can people do to train themselves to speak more directly and honestly? What can organizations do to help?

_____
_____
_____
_____
_____
_____
_____
_____
_____
_____
_____
_____
_____
_____
_____
_____

4 Protect your own motives!

2:7 But we were gentle among you, just as a nursing *mother* **cherishes her own children. ⁸So, affectionately longing for you, we were well pleased to impart to you not only the gospel of God, but also our own lives, because you had become dear to us. ⁹For you remember, brethren, our labor and toil; for laboring night and day, that we might not be a burden to any of you, we preached to you the gospel of God.**

Pure motives must be maintained at any leadership level—otherwise you won't have anyone left to lead!

Motives are the most important thing to people who are being led by someone. If people think impure motives are present, it is a "deal breaker." More often than not, everything keeps going the way it was (at least it seems that way to the leader) but the important feeling of morale is lost. A leader with questionable motives is not sensitive enough to his/her people enough to realize something is now missing.

It is essential to effective leadership that motives are protected. The Apostle Paul gives us such help in Chapter 2. In a couple of verses we are able to see how we can protect our motives through our behavior. These behaviors will both maintain pure motives and show others that leadership intentions are to lead with pure motives. Over time, those you lead will have such trust in their leader that impure motives will never come to mind.

Protect your own motives and your leadership will always be protected. Don't leave others to defend your name and reputation. Don't force people to choose sides concerning you. Nip all of this before it is ever a problem.

GENTLENESS IN EVERY SITUATION INSURES PURITY OF MOTIVE.

2:7 But we were gentle among you

In the fast moving climate of effective leadership, the idea of gentleness cannot be overlooked. It seems like there isn't time to be gentle especially when trying to motivate others to do things they may not want to do.

Gentleness is important in a completely different purpose than for motivating people. Gentleness is an important behavior for the leader. It should be an ongoing goal of development. Leadership should make the effort to be gentle in all things concerning others. In gentleness, people see the real heart of the leader rather than just the tasks that leadership wants them to do. People need to know their leader cares about them, not about what they can do for the leader.

40

Most leaders are geared toward behaviors that would be a stark contrast to gentle. This shows it is even more important for leaders to learn to be gentle.

Since gentleness is a behavior, it is acts of a person's will—not a personality type.

Gentleness does not mean passiveness either—rather, it is a true attempt from the heart of the leader to put others first and considering the life of someone else besides "me".

A NURTURER HAS A DEFINED PURPOSE— AND—A DEFINITE APPROACH.

2:7 just as a nursing *mother* cherishes her own children.

An effective leader is a nurturer—a nursing mother in whatever venue that would apply.

The nurturer is a people-developer. Remembering this point will always help you protect pure motives. The developer always sees things in light of how to develop people the best way, regardless of the circumstances before him or her..

41

Not only does a nurturer have a defined purpose (developing people) but also a definite approach. The best scenario relating to the nurturing (development) goes this way:

- **FIRST TIME—I do it and you watch me.**

- **SECOND TIME—you do it and I watch you.**

- **THIRD TIME—you do it.**

If the people you lead see that you are willing to risk your own neck for them to achieve success, they will trust you forever. If you know this about yourself, you will always prize pure motives because the desire to develop people will be a priceless treasure to you as a leader.

SHARE YOURSELF— HONESTLY AND WITH GREAT DELIGHT. IT WILL PURIFY YOUR MOTIVES AS YOU GO.

2:8 so, affectionately longing for you, we were well pleased to impart to you not only the gospel of God, but also our own lives, because you had become dear to us.

Every leader is sharing his/her life with those they serve. The investment of your life is seen in the development of you as a person and in those around you.

Hurt feelings can cause leaders to withdraw into themselves. It is important for leaders to not be discouraged by criticism, comments, or insult. A leader who fearlessly shares of themselves with others will receive the depth of respect that only comes when people see a leader opening themselves up to others.

Sharing yourself with others keeps the perspective always before you that pure motives are the only way to lead. Openness encourages everyone to keep their motives pure.

RAISE YOUR EXPECTATIONS OF GOD AND LOWER YOUR EXPECTATIONS OF PEOPLE.

2:9 for you remember, brethren, our labor and toil; for laboring night and day, that we might not be a

burden to any of you, we preached to you the gospel of God.

A huge mistake leaders make is that they have far too high of expectations for people—those who do usually have way too low of an expectation of God.

The thing to do is reverse the direction—raise your expectation of God and lower your expectation of others.

CARRY YOUR SHARE OF THE LOAD—PLUS A LITTLE MORE JUST IN CASE YOUR PERSPECTIVE OF THE LOAD IS OFF.

Most every leader feels exhausted. Many think they have the heaviest load of anyone. It may even offend them to suggest their perspective may be off just a little—but it often is—that is why you should carry just a little more of the load than what you think you should.

You will protect pure motives by always knowing you are carrying your share and not being fooled by your own energy level.

No need to get into foolish discussions with other leaders about who is doing more. Just step up and do a little more. By doing so, you will make it clear to everyone that you are not doing this for your own self-interest. It will establish your motives as pure.

If your organization needs someone to volunteer for something, step up and do so—and when you do so, set up your own perimeters of your involvement. Openness and honesty will go a long way in showing both your motives are pure and that you are balancing your life as well as your job.

Protect your own motives as you lead others. It will help both how you lead and how they trust you. Ultimately it will prevent you from losing your way as you lead others.

QUESTIONS FOR DISCUSSION

1. Explain gentleness as applied to your life.

_____

_____

_____

_____

_____

_____

2. Describe the three phases of nurturing others.

_____

_____

_____

_____

_____

_____

3. How do you share yourself?

_____

_____

_____

_____

_____

_____

4. What would you tell someone to help them expect more from God and less of others?

_____

_____

_____

_____

_____

_____

_____

_____

5 Build low-maintenance relationships!

2:10 Y ou *a re* w itnesses, a nd G od *a lso,* h ow d evoutly and justly and blamelessly we behaved ourselves among you who believe; [11]as you know how we exhorted, and comforted, and charged every one of you, as a father *does* his own children, [12]that you would walk worthy of God who calls you into His own kingdom and glory.

This is an area often overlooked among leaders. It is hard to face up to it because most leaders are interested in developing people—so they often find themselves pulled into the world of someone who ends up consuming their time and zapping their energy.

Because o f t he p otential of a n e nergy d rain, e very l eader should build low maintenance relationships with others.

Every leader goes through a super-hero stage of their leadership. This is when they really believe that if they lead in just the right way, they can help anyone grow. Before long, a leader comes to their senses and realizes you can't help a person who isn't willing to help themselves.

An effective leader will learn from the mistakes of the past. He/she w ill u nderstand t hat o ne's e nergy a nd t ime s hould b e invested into people who won't zap one's energy and time. Further, the key to the success of an organization is in the hands of the self-starters—the ones who are self-maintaining.

It is true that high-maintenance people often are the most talented and gifted people you will find. It is tempting to utilize their gifts and talents to help you succeed—**beware of this temptation! There is a tremendous downside to using people who are talented and gifted but require a huge amount of your time.** If the leader gets exhausted and then eventually burned out through high maintenance people the success will only be temporary. Worse yet, high maintenance people have a gift at skirting the responsibility if something isn't successful.

YOU CAN ACHIEVE EXTRAORDINARY SUCCESS BY USING GIFTED AND TALENTED PEOPLE— BUT—IF THEY ARE HIGH-MAINTENANCE PERSONALITIES, ALL THE SUCCESS WILL BE TEMPORARY!

You are always better off determining whether or not the people who work for you are high- or low- maintenance type people.

- **HOW MUCH TIME DO THEY REQUIRE EACH DAY?** The people around you exist to help you go farther—you don't exist to help them go farther. If you are having to keep your people hyped up—affirmed—encouraged—or happy just to get work out of them you will wear yourself out and not be effective in your leadership.

- **WHEN YOU HEAR THIS PERSON'S NAME OR SEE THEIR FACE IN YOUR MIND, DOES IT BRING YOU PAIN OR PLEASURE?** The first thought of them when you think of them is usually the thing that is really happening with your stress level in regard to them. Effective leaders can't have people around them who cause them stress. Allowing it to go on defeats the whole purpose of leadership and of leading.

- **WHEN YOU HAVE A MEETING, DO YOU HAVE TO SPEND MORE TIME AFTER YOU ADJOURN WITH ANY ONE INDIVIDUAL DISCUSSING E VENTS OF T HE M EETING?** A high-maintenance person will zap all of your time after a meeting with questions about what you said, what you thought, what you did—during the meeting. The "post meeting" required by a high-maintenance person will exceed the time spent in the meeting with everyone else. Always remember that you call a meeting so that you don't have to have individual conversations with everyone.

- **HOW MUCH PERSONAL INFORMATION IS THIS P ERSON TELLING YOU ABOUT?** There are exceptions to this rule—but in working relationships—LESS IS MORE! The high- vs. low-maintenance people are in direct proportion to the more OR less they share with you about their personal lives.

Some leaders make the huge mistake of thinking they are helping their people by counseling, advising, and staying up on what is happening in personal lives.

This is not to say people have to be distant with one another. There is a time and place for sharing—but not during company time or during the energy, productivity and creativity the organization is paying you for. When you are at work—work for your organization. If you find people not doing this, make the requirement that they take time off to get their help. **Don't be the buddy, friend, advisor, or counselor!**

The Apostle Paul presents in his own way something we can apply to our own circumstances in regard to building relationships. Chapter two, verses 10 to 12 give us some important things to watch for in others that indicate the difference between people who are high- vs. low-maintenance in building relationships.

The seven indications in these three verses help give us direction as to who are the people who will be low-maintenance people. If you see one or more of these seven things, you will know that the person you are looking at will be a low-maintenance person when you try to build a relationship with them.

Whatever you do, don't be a super-hero. If you go through the cycle where you think you can work with anyone or help anyone—try to get through it quickly! Even if you have "known someone like them" don't succumb to the temptation that if you "just listen, the person will change."

Wisdom prevails when it comes to whom to build relationships with—go for low-maintenance—whether you are dealing with your personal life or your professional life.

> # PEOPLE WHO DON'T WHINE OR COMPLAIN ARE LOW-MAINTENANCE PEOPLE—BUILD RELATIONSHIPS WITH THEM!

A person who is a whiner or complainer doesn't realize that they work it into any conversation. Listen for three minutes with anyone you meet and if they complain or whine about something, you will know they will always be a high-maintenance person.

Also when considering the first three minutes of a conversation—a person will tell you what is the most important thing to them within that short amount of time. Then listen for what they talk about the most because the thing they talk about the most is the most important thing to them.

After this kind of listening, what would you say—are they low- or high-maintenance?

```
┌─────────────────────────────────┐
│                                 │
│        PEOPLE WHO               │
│        APPEAR TO BE             │
│        FOCUSED ON WHAT          │
│        THEY WANT ARE            │
│        LOW-MAINTENANCE          │
│        PEOPLE—BUILD             │
│        RELATIONSHIPS            │
│        WITH THEM!               │
│                                 │
└─────────────────────────────────┘
```

People who know what they want are usually self-motivated in trying to achieve it. These are people you don't have to spend time with—just equip them with the tools to get the job done.

Focused people are important to an organization. They keep things going in the right direction without much interference from anyone else. They won't consume your time or zap your energy like unfocussed people will.

If you let a focused person run with what is on their mind you might not be able to use all of their stuff, but it will help your organization in many ways. An important thing is the time of the leader that is able to be used in both leading and being creative rather than in holding hands and propping people up!

> # PEOPLE WHO ARE HONEST WITH THEMSELVES ARE LOW-MAINTENANCE PEOPLE—BUILD RELATIONSHIPS WITH THEM!

The Apostle Paul's word "justly," the Greek *dikaios,* means "equitable in character."

Without coming off as suspicious—or being paranoid, ask people a couple of questions that you can check out for honesty. If you find that things were different than what they actually say, you are dealing with higher maintenance people at two different levels:

1. **The person might have forgotten and when you check it out, it won't be the same answer.** Even if this is the case—a person who can't remember conversations, assignments or events is a high-maintenance person.

2. **They might put a "spin" on their answer. When you check out what they say, you will discover some similarities to the truth, but some lacking as well.** This is another indication of a high-maintenance person. The person who puts a spin on their answer is smart enough to manipulate any situation—and hence—requires higher amounts of your time, attention and energy.

3. **They might not tell you the truth.** A person who doesn't tell the truth is a high-maintenance person. You will always be suspicious of (and you should be) every word that comes out of their mouth. You will be forced to check everything out before you believe them. This is an unnecessary use of a leader's time. All it will do is wear you out.

If you don't have the time (or opportunity) to chase down answers, there may be a couple of ways to determine whether or not the person before you is a truth teller.

Asking one or two of the following questions will help you to determine whether or not this is a high- or low- maintenance person:

- **When was the last time you made a mistake?** (A high-maintenance person won't answer this directly because nothing is ever their fault—or it will be so long ago that they will make it seem like it was someone else).

- **When was the last time you were wrong about something?** (A high-maintenance person can't answer this directly because they think they are never wrong).

- **Describe a "best friend."** (A high-maintenance person will answer this directly. You will notice them making the entire answer about them).

Although not a complete list of questions—it is a start. These types of questions will open up this important area of self-honesty in someone else's life.

PEOPLE WHO DON'T HAVE SUSPICIOUS OR QUESTIONABLE TRACK RECORDS ARE LOW-MAINTENANCE PEOPLE—BUILD RELATIONSHIPS WITH THEM!

The Apostle Paul's word "blamelessly", *amemptos* in Greek, literally means "faultless."

Our application "faultless" is more like a questionable past or suspicious behavior.

People with this kind of background will always be high-maintenance. They will either be a victim and carry baggage—

or have created problems and have issues. Although these people need help—**and this isn't to say you shouldn't help them on your personal time**—but as far as leading an organization, these people will bring a high-maintenance need. They will consume your time and wear you out. Don't let your leadership creativity and productivity be brought down by people in your organization that you are trying to help.

Help people in your personal life—not your professional life!

PEOPLE WHO HAVE PERSONAL AND PROFESSIONAL GOALS ARE LOW-MAINTENANCE PEOPLE—BUILD RELATIONSHIPS WITH THEM!

The Apostle Paul's idea of "behave" (*ginomai*) combines several modern ideas into it. The best translation for the concept he used is "to become something."

The best interpretation for us to apply it is—to set goals—personally and professionally.

People who have goals are self-starters. They can work independently. They have their own motivation to learn and grow. These personnel will require much less time and attention then those who have no goals.

You can tell who has goals just by watching them—or—by asking them what their goals are. High-maintenance people will always have something to do or take care of before they are able to set goals.

Goal setters don't have time for high-maintenance relationships either. These types of people may ask their leaders what their goals are to obtain the same kind of information. A leader should never be threatened by someone who asks this of them—they should capitalize on it and put the person to work!

PEOPLE WHO ARE POSTIVE ARE LOW-MAINTENANCE PEOPLE—BUILD RELATIONSHIPS WITH THEM!

The Apostle Paul's "we exhort and comfort—then move on" is the idea of relating encouragement to others.

It boils down this way:

Low-maintenance people are positive people—high-maintenance people are negative people.

Generalities are not an appropriate way to lead but this area would be an exception to that—if the person you are talking to is more negative than positive, then they will consume more of your time, attention and energy.

At the very least, a positive person helps you feel better about who you are and where things are going—thereby energizing you, not zapping you.

An effective leader has to find indications of behaviors any way possible. Just listening to how a person comes across is a powerful way to determine whether a future relationship should be built with another person or not.

A positive person is a hard worker. The reason this generality works is because we are not naturally positive. Human beings are prone toward the negative. A positive person has had to work hard at it.

Encouraging others requires effort -- effort that is often misinterpreted. When people try to encourage, it can often come across condescending or fake, instead being positive is a general approach that can penetrate deeper into the lives of others. So the question comes to surface: **As a leader are you more positive or more negative in your life? The same truth should be applied to yourself—the more negative you are,** the higher-maintenance of a person you will be (and vice/versa).

> # PEOPLE WHO CONDUCT THEMSELVES APPROPRIATELY ARE LOW-MAINTENANCE PEOPLE—BUILD RELATIONSHIPS WITH THEM!

"Walking worthy of God" means God is the only one we need to please. The relationship in this scenario is that of how we conduct ourselves appropriate to people and situations. If a person makes you feel awkward or uncomfortable—they will be high-maintenance for you. If you see them act inappropriately they will be high-maintenance in your organization.

QUESTIONS FOR DISCUSSION

1. Explain what high-maintenance means in relationship to leadership.

    _____

    _____

    _____

    _____

    _____

2. Explain what low-maintenance means.

    _____

    _____

    _____

    _____

    _____

3. What is the implication of having a complainer working for you?

    _____

    _____

    _____

    _____

    _____

4. How can you tell if someone is focused?

    _____

    _____

    _____

    _____

    _____

    _____

    _____

5. How important is honesty in relationships? What is honesty a reflection of?

_____

_____

_____

_____

_____

_____

_____

6. What does it mean to be "faultless?"

_____

_____

_____

_____

_____

_____

7. How important is it if someone has goals for their personal and professional life? What is it an indication of?

_____

_____

_____

_____

_____

_____

_____

8. How do you know if you see something inappropriate in someone else's behavior?

_____

_____

_____

_____

_____

6 Fortitude!

2: 13 For this reason we also thank God without ceasing, because when you received the word of God which you heard from us, you welcomed *it* **not** *as* **the word of men, but as it is in truth, the word of God, which also effectively works in you who believe.** [14]**For you, brethren, became imitators of the churches of God which are in Judea in Christ Jesus. For you also suffered the same things from your own countrymen, just as they** *did* **from the Judeans,** [15]**who killed both the Lord Jesus and their own prophets, and have persecuted us; and they do not please God and are contrary to all men,** [16]**forbidding us to speak to the Gentiles that they may be saved, so as always to fill up** *the measure of* **their sins; but w rath has come upon them to the uttermost.**

Fortitude is the ability to stick with something when things start to get tough.

Every effective leader has fortitude—that is what separates leaders from effective leaders.

Fortitude is not something any one is born with—it is a developed trait through a person's own desire and application of key concepts. It is also something that starts small and grows strong.

Experienced leaders are able to look at difficult situations as opportunities for growth because it has happened to them at countless times.

Novice leaders are often too caught up in their situation to be able to seize the moment in this way—that is why the Apostle Paul helps us see the importance of building fortitude in leadership. It is the "endurance idea" of the leadership game. Paul relates six things we can do to help us build fortitude on a day to day basis.

The idea is if we keep these six things active and working for us—we will achieve fortitude in the tough situations.

BUILDING FORTITUDE:

Be Thankful For Everything!

2:13For this reason we also thank God without ceasing,

When a person is thankful for everything, they are developing a built-in reason for everything—which is the common question that diminishes fortitude: **Why is this happening to me?**

The more you ask why—the more you will be frustrated—because you can never figure out why it is happening. Plus, when you are asking why, you are generalizing the feeling that you don't have this conflict coming. The subsequent emotion will chisel away at your strength and deeply diminish your fortitude.

On the other hand, if you are thankful for every circumstance and situation, you will exercise an important option always available to you if you let it—the option of building fortitude through every circumstance.

Thankfulness reminds you that everything is happening for a reason.

BUILDING FORTITUDE:

BUILD YOUR FOUNDATION ON A PERMANENT GUIDE FOR YOUR LIFE— GOD'S WORD!

2:13 because when you received the word of God which you heard from us, you welcomed *it* not *as* the

word of men, but as it is in truth, the word of God, which also effectively works in you who believe.

Building fortitude requires a leader to have a solid, consistent guide book. The best guide is God's Word, the Bible.

Through Bible stories, Bible principles, and Bible verses—a leader's personal and professional life can be guided in any situation they may face. A leader who commits him/herself to develop their life and leadership according to the Bible will have the fortitude necessary and the strength to draw from in facing any situation.

BUILDING FORTITUDE:

DO GOOD THINGS AND IMITATE ONLY GOOD THINGS!

2:14For you, brethren, became imitators of the churches of God which are in Judea in Christ Jesus. For you also suffered the same things from your own countrymen, just as they *did* from the Judeans,

Fortitude and building fortitude into your life requires one very major thing—

No matter what others do or say, your reaction to what they do and say will always be good.

BUILDING FORTITUDE:

THERE ARE ALWAYS GOING TO BE ENEMIES, OPPOSITION, AND CONFLICT—BUT—ALL OF IT EXISTS TO HELP ME BUILD FORTITUDE IN MY LIFE!

[2:15]who killed both the Lord Jesus and their own prophets, and have persecuted us; and they do not please God and are contrary to all men,

Every one is going to have opposition at some level. Every leader has conflict in some form or another. There might even be an enemy or two that surfaces—and this is for those leaders who are a little more "passive" in personality! Leaders with strong personalities can have great levels of all this.

No matter how intense it is, a leader sees it as an opportunity to build one's fortitude. This belief will go a long way in facing it in life.

> # BUILDING FORTITUDE:
>
> # THE BELIEF THAT WHATEVER THE SITUATION—IT WILL WORK OUT!

[2:16]**forbidding us to speak to the Gentiles that they may be saved, so as always to fill up *the measure of* their sins; but wrath has come upon them to the uttermost.**

Fortitude requires hope. The hope a leader clings on to is the belief that everything is going to work out. Whatever it is you face today will work out soon.

Effective leaders look ahead to a week, a month, six months, and even a year to think in terms of how the things that is causing them trouble will look in the future.

"Everything is going to be okay" has got to be more than a platitude—but a heartfelt and stirring belief on the part of a leader!

BUILDING FORTITUDE:

KEEP DOING WHAT YOU ARE DOING—NO MATTER HOW MESSED UP SOMETHING IS (OR GETS) THERE IS ALWAYS A POINT OF CORRECTION AHEAD IF YOU JUST KEEP WORKING IT!

No matter how messed up something is—or something gets—you can work your way through it—if—you just keep working your way through it.

The need for fortitude is when things need correction. Most of the time we don't know things are messed up until it needs fixed. It is at this point most leaders want to quit. If a leader could apply this concept rather than quit—fortitude would always be part of your life.

Regardless of the situation there is always a point of correction to get everything back on track—it is up ahead—the only way to get there is through consistently doing what you are doing right now!

Not only will you get where you need to go—you will be building fortitude all along the way.

QUESTIONS FOR DISCUSSION

1. Explain and describe fortitude.

_____

_____

_____

_____

_____

_____

_____

_____

_____

_____

2. Explain the six ways you can build fortitude in your life—give some personal and practical examples.

_____

_____

_____

_____

_____

_____

_____

_____

_____

_____

_____

_____

_____

_____

_____

_____

_____

7 Take the high road!

2:17 But we, brethren, having been taken away from you for a short time in presence, not in heart, endeavored more eagerly to see your face with great desire. [18]Therefore we wanted to come to you—even I, Paul, time and again—but Satan hindered us. [19]For what *is* our hope, or joy, or crown of rejoicing? *Is it* not even you in the presence of our Lord Jesus Christ at His coming? [20]For you are our glory and joy.

3:1 Therefore, when we could no longer endure it, we thought it good to be left in Athens alone, [2]and sent Timothy, our brother and minister of God, and our fellow laborer in the gospel of Christ, to establish you and encourage you concerning your faith, [3]that no one should be shaken by these afflictions; for you yourselves know that we are appointed to this. [4]For, in fact, we told you before when we were with you that we would suffer tribulation, just as it happened, and you know. [5]For this reason, when I could no longer endure it, I sent to know your faith, lest by some means the tempter had tempted you, and our labor might be in vain.

The idea of "the high road" is a visual description of a thought. Rather than reacting to something—the idea of the high road—is to keep your mouth shut and your attitude positive while you are processing to what is happening to you and around you.

What does "High Road mean?"

Instead of reacting to something:

- *I keep my mouth shut.*
- *I maintain a positive attitude.*
- *I take the time to process what is happening to me or around me.*

The Apostle Paul gives us some instruction in taking the high road in the situations we face. If taking the high road was ever of importance, it is in the arena of leadership. Every leader should take the high road in every circumstance.

The end of chapter two and the beginning of chapter three of 1 Thessalonians helps us in this regard. There are seven basic things we can study and apply that will help us in our attempt to always take the high road in every situation.

> # The "HIGH ROAD"
> # requires always staying
> # flexible.

2:17But we, brethren, having been taken away from you for a short time in presence, not in heart, endeavored more eagerly to see your face with great desire.

If a leader isn't flexible he/she will always be frustrated.

Controlling people often find it difficult to be flexible—but even they need to understand there are many things you can't control—(plus, it could be an excellent way in trying to break this tendency).

Keeping yourself flexible when facing every day will help you manage much of the stress that comes from trying to get every thing in and every thing done.

Most leaders would say that learning to be flexible is the key to success in any endeavor.

> # The "HIGH ROAD" requires viewing anything that appears to hinder or change your plans as a divine opportunity.

[18]**Therefore we wanted to come to you—even I, Paul, time and again—but Satan hindered us.**

A leader knows that at any second, something will come along to change plans. Sometimes people have worked on those same plans a long time. Yet, in a moment's notice, it all changes.

When a leader takes the high road, the thing that changes is not a hindrance or a pain—but a divine opportunity.

There is nothing wrong with making plans—it is what leaders are supposed to do. The need to take the high road is the understanding that no matter how much time or energy I have invested in this plan—it is going to have to change—because things have changed. **It has to be turned over to God.**

The "HIGH ROAD" requires never losing sight of hope.

[19]For what *is* our hope, or joy, or crown of rejoicing? *Is it* not even you in the presence of our Lord Jesus Christ at His coming?

A Christian has a powerful promise that includes:

- **Eternal life—a place of eternal fulfillment in the presence of God.**

- **Peace when "your time comes"—because of eternal life, God is there to see you through the most difficult time of your life.**

- **Joy in this present life in face of all your circumstances.**

In light of this promise—a Christian (especially a Christian leader) should approach every single day with a deep and abiding hope for this moment, for today, and for tomorrow.

> # The "HIGH ROAD" requires that we choose to enjoy—not be frustrated by—people.

[20]**For you are our glory and joy.**

It is a little too intense to say—but has to be said, so it is placed in some regard—but—**if you don't have people involved, you won't have any work to do. If you don't have any work to do, you won't have a job.**

Every organization needs people! People can be frustrating, lazy, silly, and even stupid. If you are going to take the high road in regard to people—you have to choose to enjoy them.

Enjoying people is a choice. You can choose to enjoy them or be frustrated by them. **The result is based solely on this choice.**

Look for the best in the people you are around and you are sure to enjoy them. Look for the worst in the people you are around and you will be frustrated continually.

> # The "HIGH ROAD" requires that we look for the best in every situation.

[20]For you are our glory and joy.

The only way to get things working for you is by making the choice to see things differently in your life and in your leadership.

The way to see things differently is by taking the time to look at the situations you face in a positive way. The high road is to look for the best in every situation you face.

There is good in the worst of every situation and bad in the best of every situation. **What you choose to look for is what you are going to find.**

This high road helps in a lot of ways. When you look for the best in every situation you will be a better leader in the situation—because you will be able to see the options better. When you are looking at the worst in the situation, you are tuned into solving problems, creating options, and moving on. This all changes when you choose to look at the best in every situation. When you do—you will take the high road and become a problem solver.

> ## The "HIGH ROAD" requires that you be an encourager regardless of how you personally feel.

[3:1]Therefore, when we could no longer endure it, we thought it good to be left in Athens alone, [2]and sent Timothy, our brother and minister of God, and our fellow laborer in the gospel of Christ, to establish you and encourage you concerning your faith,

Before this sounds like a prisoner sentence, remember this key thing—if you don't feel very well, encouraging others will cause you to be encouraged yourself as well. That is the whole idea why this will help you take the high road.

If you aren't feeling good (or good about yourself), reach out to others. It will literally change how you feel about yourself.

Especially during those times you are feeling sorry for yourself—reaching out to others will pull you out of the fog of self-pity.

> # The "HIGH ROAD" requires that you find the place with in yourself where you can be positive as a person and stay there.

[3]that no one should be shaken by these afflictions; for you yourselves know that we are appointed to this. [4]For, in fact, we told you before when we were with you that we would suffer tribulation, just as it happened, and you know. [5]For this reason, when I could no longer endure it, I sent to know your faith, lest by some means the tempter had tempted you, and our labor might be in vain.

When you are the most positive--What are you thinking about? What things can you do to maintain that mindset all the time? A positive attitude is simply a decision and an application to do so—find that place for you and keep it!

QUESTIONS FOR DISCUSSION

1. Define what "High Road" means and make some personal applications.

   _____
   _____
   _____
   _____
   _____
   _____
   _____
   _____
   _____

2. How does a person stay flexible?

   _____
   _____
   _____

3. When was the last time you were "hindered?" What should your attitude be when it happens?

   _____
   _____
   _____
   _____

4. Explain how to find the place where you can be the most positive.

   _____
   _____
   _____

8 Go all the way—<u>FORGET</u> "meet me halfway!"

3:6 But now that Timothy has come to us from you, and brought us good news of your faith and love, and that you always have good remembrance of us, greatly desiring to see us, as we also *to see* you—⁷therefore, brethren, in all our affliction and distress we were comforted concerning you by your faith. ⁸For now we live, if you stand fast in the Lord. ⁹For what thanks can we render to God for you, for all the joy with which we rejoice for your sake before our God, ¹⁰night and day praying exceedingly that we may see your face and perfect what is lacking in your faith?¹¹Now may our God and Father Himself, and our Lord Jesus Christ, direct our way to you. ¹²And may the Lord make you increase and abound in love to one another and to all, just as we *do* to you, ¹³so that He may establish your hearts blameless in holiness before our God and Father at the coming of our Lord Jesus Christ with all His saints.

Expecting too much of people is a huge mistake many leaders make.

Leaders generally have drive, passion, and desire to see things through. People who follow don't have the same level of drive, passion, and desire (or they would be leading too!) The difference between the intensity of leadership and the lack of it in people often creates a sense of frustration for a leader.

Frustration can cause a leader to do and say things that are hard to reverse—it can make a leader feel self-justified and even passionate about the lack of drive in their people.

Many leaders have become neutralized or even ineffective because they are too hard on their people. Some of the extending problems include:

- **Leaders who are neutralized rarely realize they are—their own people have learned how to neutralize them behind their backs—without the leader's knowledge of it.**

- **Leaders who are frustrated become so self-justified that they replace person after person after person with no regard that the problem might be with them personally.**

- **Leaders can become so intense that they create their own sense of reality—with expectations so high of others that they could never achieve them.**

- **Leaders often put more on themselves then what is necessary when people don't respond in the way they expect—thereby creating undo stress and pressure for everyone.**

Effective leaders find a way to be fulfilled and passionate without n eeding t o control t he p eople t hey l ead—or examine too closely what the response has been to their leadership.

A leader will never be satisfied with how people respond to his/her leadership because expectation is dictated by their own passion and intensity.

What should a leader do? Create a sense of personal intensity that is not related in any way to expectation of others—only expectation of self.

Go all the way—don't expect anyone to meet you half way.

The Apostle Paul relates to us how we can create a place in our leadership that is self-balancing. We can lead others and be personally fulfilled without needing to relate to their following us as a basis of our personal affirmation.

Leaders need a space created between their frustration and their reaction. Working these five things can help. If you go "all the way" in developing these things for your life you will find yourself more focused on your tasks rather than consumed by your frustrations. This will help balance the expectation you have of others. If you go all the way with five important things—and put your intensity into them—you will turn the expectation you have of others into personal and professional success not tied in any way to the productivity of others.

GO ALL THE WAY WITH HOLDING ON TO YOUR JOY!

Assert yourself as a leader into any situation without having to put your conditions on someone else.

---

^{3:6}**But now that Timothy has come to us from you, and brought us good news of your faith and love, and that you always have good remembrance of us, greatly desiring to see us, as we also *to see* you.**

It may be hard to realize because most people think joy is some emotional "high" to get when you are feeling good. The truth is certain about joy being a deeply spiritual assurance that everything is fine—everything is going to work out—and you can be happy regardless of any circumstance. Joy is something you hold on to because you want to!

GO ALL THE WAY CALM YOURSELF DOWN!

Look for others who are worked up and help them to calm down—if you can't calm them down—remind yourself that is how you are when you won't calm down.

[7]therefore, brethren, in all our affliction and distress we were comforted concerning you by your faith.

When your expectation of people is too high, you will always be worked up—they will never meet your expectations—and you will be miserable.

Calming down is a decision. People can help by assuring, reassuring and affirming you—but if you don't make a decision to calm down you will keep going back until someone else comes along to calm you down.

> ## <u>GO ALL THE WAY</u>
> ## COVER YOURSELF UP WITH A POSITIVE ATTITUDE!
>
> **Let a positive attitude be with you wherever you go and whenever you speak. Further, let it always be in your mind.**

[9]For what thanks can we render to God for you, for all the joy with which we rejoice for your sake before our God, [10]night and day praying exceedingly that we may see your face and perfect what is lacking in your faith?

A positive attitude is always possible if you are conscious of it. A leader who has a high expectation of others also has the ability to change up his/her intensity and place it into something else. Instead of the frustration that comes from the expectation of others, try focusing that same energy into thinking positive thoughts all the time. Look for the best, think about the best, and concentrate on the best/positive things. Doing so will "cover" you in a positive attitude.

<u>GO ALL THE WAY</u> EXPRESS APPRECIATION FOR WHO YOU ARE AND WHAT YOU HAVE!

Allow the energy created by doing this to propel you beyond the call of duty. Do so without needing to expect it in others.

---

[9]For what thanks can we render to God for you, for all the joy with which we rejoice for your sake before our God, [10]night and day praying exceedingly that we may see your face and perfect what is lacking in your faith?

GO ALL THE WAY
STAY OPEN!

Keep your mind open. Listen to what others are thinking, saying and doing. They may not communicate directly so watch carefully.

[11]Now may our God and Father Himself, and our Lord Jesus Christ, direct our way to you. [12]And may the Lord make you increase and abound in love to one another and to all, just as we *do* to you, [13]so that He may establish your hearts blameless in holiness before our God and Father at the coming of our Lord Jesus Christ with all His saints.

Staying open prevents stubbornness—which is a real neutralizer for leadership effectiveness. Always be open for ideas—don't make presumptions.

The key to preventing leadership frustration is to go all out and all the way yourself—without putting that same level of intensity on those you work with. This can take some discipline, but it will always pay off in the end.

If you can't keep from demanding your own way or creating a need to control others, you will be able to put that energy into going all the way yourself.

Frustration requires energy that could better serve your organization. Harness it! Put your emotional energy into positive things that will better lead others and serve your organization.

GO ALL THE WAY. DON'T EXPECT OTHERS TO MEET YOU HALFWAY!

QUESTIONS FOR DISCUSSION

1. Explain how leaders get frustrated.

    _____

    _____

    _____

    _____

    _____

2. How does "joy" help in the life and work of a leader?

    _____

    _____

    _____

    _____

3. Explain how to calm yourself down.

    _____

    _____

    _____

    _____

4. What does it mean to "cover yourself up in a positive attitude?

    _____

    _____

5. How does staying open help in leadership?

    _____

    _____

    _____

9 Stay up to date with everyone and everything!

4:1 Finally then, brethren, we urge and exhort in the Lord Jesus that you should abound more and more, just as you received from us how you ought to walk and to please God; [2]for you know what commandments we gave you through the Lord Jesus.[3]For this is the will of God, your sanctification: that you should abstain from sexual immorality; [4]that each of you should know how to possess his own vessel in sanctification and honor, [5]not in passion of lust, like the Gentiles who do not know God; [6]that no one should take advantage of and defraud his brother in this matter, because the Lord *is* the avenger of all such, as we also forewarned you and testified. [7]For God did not call us to uncleanness, but in holiness. [8]Therefore he who rejects *this* does not reject man, but God, who has also given us His Holy Spirit.[9]But concerning brotherly love you have no need that I should write to you, for you yourselves are taught by God to love one another; [10]and indeed you do so toward all the brethren who are in all Macedonia. But we urge you, brethren, that you increase more and more; [11]that you also aspire to lead a quiet life, to mind your own business, and to work with your own hands, as we commanded you, [12]that you may walk properly toward those who are outside, and *that* you may lack nothing.

Staying up to date with people and situations takes much effort on the part of anyone—but can be especially difficult for a leader.

A leader is often caught in the hustle and bustle of leading, thereby letting go of many essentials such as staying up to date with people or situations along the way.

It is often after a crisis that people realize their need to live up to date with those they love—but over time go back to their old habits. Staying up to date in relationships is a daily investment of time and energy. When the days become weeks—almost always the weeks will become months.

It doesn't have to be New Year's resolution every year. It should be a change of lifestyle that dictates "I am going to start staying up to date with people and situations."

The Apostle Paul gives us some help in coming to terms with staying up to date. These concepts go a long way in keeping us accountable so it isn't just something we say we are going to do—but it is something we follow through on.

The basic idea is to be aware of your surroundings, not just what you are focused on getting done. This awareness will help you to begin to see that there is more to the "picture" than what has to be done—but also how you are going to get it done—who is going to be involved in getting it done—how will others be affected while getting it done—and—how important are each of these to each other.

Leaders need focus but the more focused a leader becomes, the more balanced they should become as well. The balance will help the leader to stay up to date with people and situations.

> **KEEP DOING WHAT YOU ARE DOING THE BEST—AND MOST COMPLETE WAY YOU CAN—UNTIL THIS DOOR CLOSES. (THEN THE NEXT DOOR WILL OPEN FOR YOU).**

Leaders can take themselves so seriously that they become confused as to what they should be doing. They over-compensate for the confusion by blocking out the people and situations around them (as if it all was the "enemy").

When things begin to break down, the natural tendency is to run. A leader caught into this kind of mentality needs to keep doing what they are doing and things will become clearer as they work through it.

The more a leader works, the more the need to stay up to date will become. Many times a leader will work up a storm—feel rejected—and find another job. Some leaders do this with their relationships as well. This kind of reaction has to have its cycle broken. The only way to break it is to see everything as God's open door. The idea should be: "I am going to work at this as God's open door until he shuts this door and opens a new one."

If you allow yourself to see the divine work in it, you will be less likely to bolt when things get tough. You will also tend to realize the only way to do a complete job is to keep up to date with relationships and with situations you face. If you don't stay up to date in this way—things will get backed up on you.

Extending the idea of a divine directive—a leader must believe they are where they are supposed to be right now. If a leader can believe this, then many of the things the leader tries to control or fix aren't as important as making sure people and situations are up to date.

It is important to take an inventory several times through a day asking yourself—

- **"Am I up to date with people I love?"**

- **"Am I up to date with the people I work with?"**

- **"Am I up to date in the situations I am facing?"**

TAKE CONTROL OF YOUR THOUGHTS— THEN YOUR VALUES— THEN YOUR MORALS—AND THEN YOUR LIFE.

Taking control of your thoughts requires the will do to so. It is simply done by wanting to AND desiring to be accountable for your thoughts.

Start off by targeting certain thoughts you don't want to be part of your life. When you catch yourself—visualize yourself bombing it out of existence—see it vaporize in your mind. This will help you see and understand that your thoughts don't have to rage out of control, but can be captured and destroyed.

Once you have trained yourself to take control of your thoughts—it will give way to thinking through the things you value—and how you value them.

Your sense of value will help you think through your personal morals and moral standards that you believe for your life.

Finally, you are able to take control of your life—which will help you to stay up to date in your relationships and situations.

NO REGRETS!
LIVE YOUR LIFE
WITHOUT HOLDING
ON TO ANY KIND OF
REGRET.

Living life with no regrets would seem to be a natural outgrowth of staying up to date. In this case, it is an attempt to staying up to date in a practical way.

If any level of regret is present in your life it won't be possible to stay up to date. It will always be obstacle until it is resolved. As are all the rest of these concepts, living life with no regret is a decision of a person's own will. You live your life with no regret if you want to.

A leader has to live life with no regret to be effective personally and professionally.

MIND YOUR OWN BUSINESS.

It will help you keep your energy level managed properly—and it will keep tension and conflict to a minimum.

Sticking your nose into someone else's business is what creates much of the conflict between people.

An important way to stay up to date is to not cause yourself more work—by minding your own business.

Involving yourself in the business of others often causes tension and stress between people and zaps the energy of a leader. Why put yourself through all of this? Just mind your own business!

TAKE OFF YOUR MASK AND BE REAL WITH PEOPLE IN EVERY SITUATION!

Let people know who you really are by being real with them.

Most people feel that rejection will result from taking off one's mask. If you don't risk it—you won't be really staying up to date with people and situations—you will only be staying up to date in a fake sort of way.

If you are real with people, you will be respected. People won't always agree with you but they will appreciate you for who you are.

It is true that some people won't like the real you—but that is much better than them liking the fake side of you—which would be a lie!

Trust others enough to be yourself—it is the ultimate way to stay up to date.

QUESTIONS FOR DISCUSSION

Discuss what it means to stay up to date with people and situations—then apply the five things discussed in this chapter to your own life:

_____

_____

_____

_____

_____

_____

_____

_____

_____

_____

_____

_____

_____

_____

_____

_____

_____

_____

_____

_____

_____

_____

_____

_____

_____

_____

_____

10 Build at every opportunity!

4:13 But I do not want you to be ignorant, brethren, concerning those who have fallen asleep, lest you sorrow as others who have no hope. [14]For if we believe that Jesus died and rose again, even so God will bring with Him those who sleep in Jesus.[15]For this we say to you by the word of the Lord, that we who are alive *and* remain until the coming of the Lord will by no means precede those who are asleep. [16]For the Lord Himself will descend from heaven with a shout, with the voice of an archangel, and with the trumpet of God. And the dead in Christ will rise first. [17]Then we who are alive *and* remain shall be caught up together with them in the clouds to meet the Lord in the air. And thus we shall always be with the Lord. [18]Therefore comfort one another with these words.

5:1But concerning the times and the seasons, brethren, you have no need that I should write to you. [2]For you yourselves know perfectly that the day of the Lord so comes as a thief in the night. [3]For when they say, "Peace and safety!" then sudden destruction comes upon t hem, a s l abor p ains u pon a p regnant w oman. And they shall not escape. [4]But you, brethren, are not in darkness, so that this Day should overtake you as a thief. [5]You are all sons of light and sons of the day. We are not of the night nor of darkness. [6]Therefore let us not sleep, as others *do,* but let us watch and be sober. [7]For those who sleep, sleep at night, and those who get drunk are drunk at night. [8]But let us who are of the day be sober, putting on the breastplate of faith and love, and *as* a helmet the hope of salvation. [9]For God did not appoint us to wrath, but to obtain salvation through our Lord Jesus Christ, [10]who died for us, that whether we wake or sleep, we should live together with Him.[11]Therefore comfort each other and edify one another, just as you also are doing.

The purpose of leadership is to build the organization—the only way to build the organization is by building those people associated with the organization. **If you don't build the people in the organization, you will have an organization to build!**

The leader who is a builder trains to do/be so. The effort required is to look beyond yourself and into those you serve and work with. The bottom line is **"I succeed if they succeed."** The question that follows is: **"How can I help them succeed?"**

<u>Every Leader Should Think:</u> "I succeed if they succeed"—<u>And Ask:</u> "How can I help them succeed?"

The training in building others up requires a conscious and diligent effort applied like a template until these skills are acquired and come naturally in the course of your day.

The Apostle Paul gives us some teaching on the "how to build others up" from chapters 4 and 5 of 1 Thessalonians. Before we get that teaching—it is important to deal with how leaders need to be more conscious of building others up. First, let's look at plans to quick start your consciousness to build others up. Then we'll look at Paul's ideas on how to build others up through a leadership model.

> # TRAINING IS REQUIRED TO BUILD OTHERS UP. USE THE TRAINING AS A TEMPLATE UNTIL YOU ACQUIRE THE SKILL.

Developing a Consciousness of Building Others Up:

- **Build a moment or pause four times into your day where you ask yourself: "Have I been building others up?"**
- **Right after being with someone, make it a habit to ask yourself: "Did I build that person up?"**

Take this training in consciousness seriously, but don't become frustrated. It is better to work at this concept by seeing its importance. Eventually, this will establish it as important in your mind.

If you are not consciously aware of how and when you are helping to develop and build the character of others, your efforts may appear insincere and become counterproductive. A leader who is building others up by faking it will be seen as less than genuine and won't be trusted by others.

The Apostle Paul's ideas are simple, yet profound if you apply them to your leadership. If you mess up or forget—start over and apply them. Being an effective leader doesn't mean you are a perfect leader. We all learn on the job. Use Paul's teaching as a check list if it helps you build others up—or work on one for a while—then another—and so forth.

The leader who works at building others will find their whole world becoming better because learning and applying these concepts will extend to one's personal life. We need to also be leaders in our homes. Building up our loved ones is a primary need in the family unit. If family members aren't built up, they will feel beaten up.

Leadership is not a faucet you turn on and off—either you lead or you don't—it will affect every area of your life.

What you will find is that one or more of these ideas will be more natural to apply—so go with it! A leader doesn't have to master all five of these ideas. Apply the natural ones or the easier ones for you—then work on the tougher ones. It is more important for a leader to work on building others up by being conscious of the need and the desire to do it. This kind of attitude will be more powerful than the actual application.

1. INSTILL HOPE IN OTHERS!

Let others know there is always hope in every circumstance.

There is always a solution to every problem. Even when there doesn't seem to be an answer, remind people that they feel that way right now—and the feeling is only temporary—there is an answer; it just hasn't come to us yet!

Remind people that the best days to experience are not behind—but ahead.

Always listen to yourself say these things. They apply to everyone, but especially to the leader saying them. If you listen to yourself you will begin to see the importance of building others up.

Most of the time, all people need is hope instilled into their situation. They need simple affirmation that everything is going to turn out for the best.

People drink up hope like they are dying of thirst in a desert! They are desperate to know their work (and especially their life) has meaning. Their deepest need is to make a difference in their life and world. Their leader can give them that through instilling hope into their life.

2. RAISE THE BAR! Don't treat people like they are fragile or they will feel weak and under-valued.

Challenging people is one of the best ways to build them up. Building up others involves treating them like they are powerful in their own right and have an unlimited potential for success.

This means you have to challenge them with greatness. Don't pat people on top of the heads—raise the bar for them so they know you know nothing is impossible for them to accomplish.

Challenging people doesn't mean passing on your personal agenda or organizational goals on to them. It means to instill in them personally a sense of greatness—that they have the personal ability to have an unlimited potential in their life—not connected in any way to what will help you achieve greatness in your organization.

Rallying people to a sense of greatness in their organization is not raising the bar at all—it is self-serving—and self defeating if you don't achieve all of your organizational strategy. Build people individually and personally and you will build your organization.

3. BLAZE YOUR OWN PATH AND LEAVE A POSITIVE, WELL-LIGHTED TRAIL FOR OTHERS TO FOLLOW!

A leader who builds others up is sought out by other people.

The key is to build others up without desiring affirmation yourself from their personal reaction to your effort. If you are building someone up and being personally encouraged by their reaction, you will always be disappointed. People will never give you the sense of acceptance (or satisfaction on your part) that you are looking for.

A leader must blaze his/her own path for others to follow. You have to resolve and desire to build up people for the reasons already touched on and then proceed— and try not be affected by their reaction.

The path you blaze needs to be a positive one (so it will encourage others to follow) and a well-lit one (well communicated to others).

4. KEEP YOUR OPINIONS TO YOURSELF—EVEN IF YOU ARE ASKED!

THE OPINIONS OF THE LEADER ENDS UP MAKING PEOPLE BOTH FEEL NERVOUS AND BECOME SECOND-GUESSERS.

A leader's personal opinions do not help to build up and develop others. It just makes the people around you tentative in their approach to you (and their job). A leader can't afford to have his/her people tentative.

Build people up without having to share opinion. Lead them without being opinion-based and you will build a richer, deeper organization and higher-minded, sincere people around you.

5. COMPLEMENT THE GOOD THINGS AND KEEP YOUR MOUTH SHUT OTHERWISE— (THEY WILL GET THE MESSAGE).

You can make this assumption: **MOST OF THE TIME PEOPLE KNOW WHEN THEY HAVE MESSED UP.** Pointing it out to them doesn't build it up—it just "wipes their noses into it" and thereby defeats your desire to build them up.

Complement people in specific areas. It is better to be specific rather than a general (and insincere) "nice job on that." The insincerity this brings creates a distrust of leadership. People know when something isn't right—give them the time and space to deal with it themselves. Center in on what they did right and build that up.

QUESTIONS FOR DISCUSSION

1. Name the two levels needed in a leader's thinking to build others up.

_____

_____

_____

_____

_____

_____

_____

2. Name one of the five things to build others up discussed in the chapter that you have applied to your life and leadership and explain.

_____

_____

_____

_____

_____

_____

_____

3. Name one of the five things to build others up that you are bad at or messed up on and how you could/can do better.

_____

_____

_____

_____

_____

_____

_____

11 Responsibilities of Leadership!

5:12 And we urge you, brethren, to recognize those who labor among you, and are over you in the Lord and admonish you, [13]and to esteem them very highly in love for their work's sake. Be at peace among yourselves.[14]Now we exhort you, brethren, warn those who are unruly, comfort the fainthearted, uphold the weak, be patient with all. [15]See that no one renders evil for evil to anyone, but always pursue what is good both for yourselves and for all.[16]Rejoice always, [17]pray without ceasing, [18]in everything give thanks; for this is the will of God in Christ Jesus for you.[19]Do not quench the Spirit. [20]Do not despise prophecies. [21]Test all things; hold f ast w hat is good. [22]Abstain f rom every form of evil.[23]Now may the God of peace Himself sanctify you completely; and may your whole spirit, soul, and body be preserved blameless at the coming of our Lord Jesus Christ. [24]He who calls you *is* faithful, who also will do *it*.[25]Brethren, pray for us.[26]Greet all the brethren with a holy kiss.[27]I charge you by the Lord that this epistle be read to all the holy brethren.[28]The grace of our Lord Jesus Christ *be* with you. Amen.

The Apostle Paul relays to leaders in the final verses of chapter 5—1 Thessalonians—an often repeated teaching that he used in his entire ministry to help (and train) leaders to be effective.

The areas here may be repetitious in concept—even then—every leader should keep thinking, analyzing, and applying these concepts to their personal and professional lives.

This time, it is eleven areas of interest. Use these as a checklist and challenge list. Don't be sorry, guilty, emotional, or defensive when looking them over. Let them speak for themselves—don't make yourself have to speak for them or defend yourself regarding them.

"It is what it is" and these eleven concepts are what they are—responsibilities of leadership.

RECOGNIZE PEOPLE:
- **Their work.**
- **Their identity.**
- **Their presence.**

---

[12]And we urge you, brethren, to recognize those who labor among you, and are over you in the Lord and admonish you.

HOLD PEOPLE IN HIGH ESTEEM:

- **By how you treat them.**
- **By how you talk to them.**
- **By what you say about them behind their backs.**

[13] Esteem them very highly in love for their work's sake.

KEEP PEACE—<u>if you can</u>—(the best way you can).

[13] Be at peace among yourselves.

**DON'T BE PASSIVE—
things won't just take
care of themselves!**

- **Confront and guide
  people who are
  causing trouble.**
- **Give people the
  attention they are
  craving.**
- **Have people repeat
  back to you what
  they have heard you
  say. (Prevent
  misunderstanding)**

[14]Now we exhort you, brethren, warn those who are
unruly.

STRENGTHEN THOSE WHO ARE WEAK BY GUIDING AND HELPING.

(Verse 14) "Comfort the fainthearted, uphold the weak"

THE MOST IMPORTANT WORD IN LEADERSHIP RESPONSIBILITY IS—PATIENCE.

(Verse 14) be patient with all.

> # THE RESPONSIBILITY OF LEADERSHIP IS THE <u>ACCEPTANCE</u> OF THE RESPONSIBILITY OF LEADERSHIP.
> ## In a Phrase:
> ## <u>"Not under my watch!"</u>

[15]See that no one renders evil for evil to anyone, but always pursue what is good both for yourselves and for all.

> # ALWAYS REJOICE! IT IS A CHOICE.

[16]Rejoice always

THE MOST IMPORTANT MEETING OF THE DAY FOR A LEADER: YOUR OWN PERSONAL PRAYER MEETING!

---

[17]pray without ceasing

KEEP AN OPEN MIND TO OTHER POINTS OF VIEW—BUT—AT THE SAME TIME, CHECK EVERYTHING OUT!

---

[18]in everything give thanks; for this is the will of God in Christ Jesus for you.[19]Do not quench the Spirit. [20]Do not despise prophecies. [21]Test all things; hold fast what is good. [22]Abstain from every form of evil.

THE ULTIMATE RESPONSIBILITY OF THE LEADER IS TO TEACH OTHERS—SO—ALWAYS BE A TEACHER!

(THE MOST EFFECTIVE TEACHER IS THE ONE WHO IS FIRST A STUDENT).

[23]Now may the God of peace Himself sanctify you completely; and may your whole spirit, soul, and body be preserved blameless at the coming of our Lord Jesus Christ. [24]He who calls you *is* faithful, who also will do *it*.[5]Brethren, pray for us.[26]Greet all the brethren with a holy kiss.[27]I charge you by the Lord that this epistle be read to all the holy brethren.[28]The grace of our Lord Jesus Christ *be* with you. Amen.

QUESTIONS FOR DISCUSSION

1. What does it mean to recognize people?

   _____

   _____

   _____

2. What are the three ways to hold people in high esteem?

   _____

   _____

   _____

3. What are some ways to keep from being passive as a leader?

   _____

   _____

   _____

4. How do you strengthen someone who is weak?

   _____

   _____

   _____

5. What is the most important word in leadership?

   _____

   _____

   _____

6. What is the most important meeting of the day for a leader?

   _____

   _____

   _____

7. What is the ultimate responsibility of the leader?

   _____

   _____

   _____

12 There is always something to learn!

2 Thessalonians

[1]Paul, Silvanus, and Timothy, to the church of the Thessalonians in God our Father and the Lord Jesus Christ:[2]Grace to you and peace from God our Father and the Lord Jesus Christ.[3]We are bound to thank God always for you, brethren, as it is fitting, because your faith grows exceedingly, and the love of every one of you all abounds toward each other, [4]so that we ourselves boast of you among the churches of God for your patience and faith in all your persecutions and tribulations that you endure, [5]*which is* manifest evidence of the righteous judgment of God, that you may be counted worthy of the kingdom of God, for which you also suffer; [6]since *it is* a righteous thing with God to repay with tribulation those who trouble you, [7]and to *give* you who are troubled rest with us when the Lord Jesus is revealed from heaven with His mighty angels, [8]in flaming fire taking vengeance on those who do not know God, and on those who do not obey the gospel of our Lord Jesus Christ. [9]These shall be punished with everlasting destruction from the presence of the Lord and from the glory of His power, [10]when He comes, in that Day, to be glorified in His saints and to be admired among all those who believe, because our testimony among you was believed.[11]Therefore we also pray always for you that our God would count you worthy of *this* calling, and fulfill all the good p leasure of *His* goodness a nd the

work of faith with power, [12]that the name of our Lord Jesus Christ may be glorified in you, and you in Him, according to the grace of our God and the Lord Jesus Christ.

There is always something to learn and every effective leader learns real fast that there is always something to learn.

It could be a mantra that leaders recite driving to work and home from work:

GOING TO WORK: "I am going to learn some good things today!"

COMING HOME FROM WORK: "I sure learned some good things today!"

Just as the Apostle Paul teaches that every leader is a teacher— so also every leader is a student—a learner through out life. There is always something we can learn and Paul brings out some important things in 2 Thessalonians chapter one.

> # A LEADER MUST LEARN TO FIND THE THING THEY CAN BE THANKFUL FOR.
> # V. 1-3

A thankful attitude covers over a multitude of stress and pressure. Learning to find the thing you can be thankful for will release the pressure valve of leadership just as often as you do it!

A LEADER MUST LEARN TO GO BEYOND THE MINIMUM REQUIREMENTS AND FIND THE WAY TO EXCEED THE MAXIMUM EXPECTATION MOST OF THE TIME.
V. 3b

People who lead are generally already motivated to do their best—so it would seem to go with out saying they should exceed the minimum requirements. The thing that a leader learns is to quickly find the way to exceed expectation.

Every situation a leader faces has different expectations because there are many different dynamics involved. The desire to be a learner will go a long way in various circumstances to help a leader determine how to exceed expectation.

A LEADER MUST LEARN TO LET KINDNESS ABOUND TOWARD EVERYONE!
V. 3c

Kindness toward everyone is the greatest strategy in leadership and in life. Rather than intimidation, if people can count on you being kind, you will neutralize a huge percentage of potential leadership problems.

A LEADER MUST LEARN TO NOT JUST SURVIVE—BUT THRIVE BY PATIENTLY ENDURING.
V. 4

If a leader is just "hanging on" or "just surviving", they will be unfulfilled and exhausted all the time.

A learner is a person who doesn't just survive, but thrives. The way toward thriving is through patiently enduring. An effective leader learns quickly how to patiently endure through any tough time they face.

A LEADER MUST LEARN TO BE MOTIVATED BY ETERNAL PROMISES FOUND IN THE BIBLE—BECAUSE THAT IS OUR REASON FOR LEARNING! V. 5-10

It shouldn't surprise us that the Apostle Paul occasionally pulls out the end of times issue when dealing with leadership. It is an important process in leadership to learn that we are working toward a higher purpose—and—eternal life.

The lessons we learn—as a learner—and as a leader have eternal significance. Leaders should always be learning and studying about the impact of eternity. Doing so will enrich the leadership endeavors of today.

> # A LEADER MUST LEARN THE MOST IMPORTANT PEP TALK TO YOURSELF IS: "I AM NOT (AND NEVER WILL BE) ALONE!"
> # V. 11-12

Probably the hardest thing for a leader to learn is—"I am not alone"—because leadership is (by nature)—a lonely sojourn.

It might start that way but doesn't have to continue that way if the leader is a learner. The learning leader will reign in those lonely feelings and remind him/her that no one is ever completely alone!

126

QUESTIONS FOR DISCUSSION

1. Discuss why a leader is always a learner.

_____

_____

_____

_____

_____

_____

_____

_____

_____

_____

_____

2. Discuss the things a "leader must learn."

_____

_____

_____

_____

_____

_____

_____

_____

_____

_____

_____

_____

_____

_____

_____

_____

13 You don't have to be nervous— because it is always a choice!

2:1 Now, brethren, concerning the coming of our Lord Jesus Christ and our gathering together to Him, we ask you, [2]not to be soon shaken in mind or troubled, either by spirit or by word or by letter, as if from us, as though the day of Christ had come. [3]Let no one deceive you by any means; for *that Day will not come* unless the falling away comes first, and the man of sin is revealed, the son of perdition, [4]who opposes and exalts himself above all that is called God or that is worshiped, so that he sits as God in the temple of God, showing himself that he is God.[5]Do you not remember that when I was still with you I told you these things? [6]And now you know what is restraining, that he may be revealed in his own time. [7]For the mystery of lawlessness is already at work; only He who now restrains *will do so* until He is taken out of the way. [8]And then the lawless one will be revealed, whom the Lord will consume with the breath of His mouth and destroy with the brightness of His coming. [9]The coming of the *lawless one* is according to the working of Satan, with all power, signs, and lying wonders, [10]and with all unrighteous deception among those who perish, because they did not receive the love of the truth, that they might be saved. [11]And for this reason God will send them strong delusion, that they should believe the lie, [12]that they all may be condemned who did not believe the truth but had pleasure in unrighteousness.[13]But we are bound to give thanks to

God always for you, brethren beloved by the Lord, because God from the beginning chose you for salvation through sanctification by the Spirit and belief in the truth, [14]to which He called you by our gospel, for the obtaining of the glory of our Lord Jesus Christ. [15]Therefore, brethren, stand fast and hold the traditions which you were taught, whether by word or our epistle.[16]Now may our Lord Jesus Christ Himself, and our God and Father, who has loved us and given *us* everlasting consolation and good hope by grace, [17]comfort your hearts and establish you in every good word and work.

Nervous leaders are tentative leaders—tentative leaders never quite **SOAR** in accordance to the effectiveness to lead.

The Apostle Paul came across leaders all the time who were nervous. He often coached the first one he mentored, Timothy, on his nervous condition. He was understanding and appreciative of his people. Paul also challenged them strongly with the need to step up and realize that nervousness is a decision.

Stress is always something we can manage—when it is brought on by nervousness we must nip it in the beginning stages.

Coaches contend a certain amount of nervousness for an athlete helps them perform their event better. The reason it looks this way is because the athlete is able to do what the Apostle Paul is telling us to do: **Harness your nervousness—direct it—focus it into something positive.**

The leader who can do this will be effective in whatever area they lead. You don't have to be controlled by your fear, nerves, or stress. It is up to you!

It is up to you:
BUT YOU COULD BE A MUCH BETTER LEADER IF YOU DON'T LET YOURSELF GET "RATTLED" BY THE CIRCUMSTANCES AROUND YOU.
V. 1

Honestly, everyone gets rattled once in a while. Things can happen quickly and catch you off guard or by surprise. It is perfectly naturally to be temporarily and momentarily caught by surprise.

Pull yourself together quickly and deal with the problem facing you—get it off the table and move on to other leadership stuff.

If you ignore or put off dealing with the thing that temporarily rattled you—it will just fester internally and cause the kind of nervousness that makes a leader tentative.

> # It is up to you:
> # BUT YOU DON'T HAVE TO CARRY WORRY AROUND WITH YOU— RELEASE IT AND BE FREE FROM IT!
> # V. 2

Nervousness eventually gives way to worry. Worry can bring on emotional/mental issues that will weigh a leader down. Worry needs to be released out of your life.

How do you perform the "exorcism of worry?"

- **Visualize yourself turning the things bothering you over to God.**

- **When it comes back on you—don't let it—remind yourself that you released the thing bothering you back to God.**

- **Repeat these steps in repetition until it takes!**

> **It is up to you:**
> **KEEP YOUR EYES**
> **OPEN FOR THE**
> **THINGS THAT CAUSE**
> **YOU TO BE NERVOUS**
> **AND TOUGHEN UP BY**
> **PREPARING**
> **YOURSELF AHEAD OF**
> **TIME.**
> **V. 3**

A personal "trigger" is a thing you identify in yourself that has "pushed your button\s" or caused you to behave a certain way.

Leaders learn to identify their "triggers" quickly.

There are things that will trigger nervousness. The best way to harness or focus nervousness in positive way—the way coaches train athletes—is to identify the things that trigger nervousness for you personally and get it turned over and released ahead of time.

> # It is up to you:
> # BUT BEWARE OF PEOPLE WHO EXALT THEMSELVES—THEY WILL MAKE YOU NERVOUS AND INEFFECTIVE AS A LEADER!
> # V. 4

Certain people can make you nervous. Don't feel bad about that. Actually—go with it!

There is a reason you are nervous around or because of this person—don't fight it. Be cautious concerning them. Let the nervousness you experience being around them help you understand yourself better. People who exalt themselves are insecure. They don't feel quite affirmed enough and feel the need to project it out there. Use the experience to remind yourself that you don't have to be like that person. Plus, you don't have to be threatened—because you are seeing is insecurity in action!

> # It is up to you:
> # BUT ONCE IN A WHILE, THINGS GET PURGED— WIPED OUT—AND THIS IS A GOOD THING BECAUSE IT CAUSES US TO FIND BOTH OUR SECURITY AND DEPENDENCY ON GOD.

Let's clear it up right now—**from time to time we are all going to be wiped out and have to start over again.**

So what? It is all good.

Often we become too independent minded. We need to start over once in a while to be reminded who is in charge. The thing we fear—the thing we are nervous about—might be the best thing for us!

> **It is up to you:**
> **BUT IF YOU STAY**
> **THE COURSE—DOING**
> **WHAT YOU KNOW IS**
> **RIGHT TO DO—YOU**
> **DON'T HAVE**
> **ANYTHING IN YOUR**
> **LIFE YOU SHOULD BE**
> **NERVOUS ABOUT!**
> **V. 13-17**

If you stay the course—and it doesn't matter what course you are on—there is always a point of correction out there. It doesn't matter how bad you have messed up there is always a way to get back on track.

One thing that makes a leader nervous is thinking they have made the wrong decision and they "second guess" themselves. Remember that even if you have made the wrong decision—you still should not get nervous about it—there is always the point of correction out there a ways if you just stay the course!

QUESTIONS FOR DISCUSSION

1. Explain how nervousness is a choice.

_____
_____
_____
_____
_____
_____
_____

2. How do you let go of worry?

_____
_____
_____
_____
_____

3. Why should we beware of people who exalt themselves?

_____
_____
_____
_____

4. Why is it important to be wiped out and start over again once in a while?

_____
_____
_____
_____
_____
_____
_____

14 Work hard—and only work with those who work hard!

3:1 Finally, brethren, pray for us, that the word of the Lord may run *swiftly* and be glorified, just as *it is* with you, ²and that we may be delivered from unreasonable and wicked men; for not all have faith.³But the Lord is faithful, who will establish you and guard *you* from the evil one. ⁴And we have confidence in the Lord concerning you, both that you do and will do the things we command you.⁵Now may the Lord direct your hearts into the love of God and into the patience of Christ.⁶But we command you, brethren, in the name of our Lord Jesus Christ, that you withdraw from every brother who walks disorderly and not according to the tradition which he received from us. ⁷For you yourselves know how you ought to follow us, for we were not disorderly among you; ⁸nor did we eat anyone's bread free of charge, but worked with labor and toil night and day, that we might not be a burden to any of you, ⁹not because we do not have authority, but to make ourselves an example of how you should follow us.¹⁰For even when we were with you, we commanded you this: If anyone will not work, neither shall he e at. ¹¹For w e h ear t hat t here a re s ome w ho walk among you in a disorderly manner, not working at all, but are busybodies. ¹²Now those who are such we command and exhort through our Lord Jesus Christ that they work in quietness and eat their own bread.¹³But *as for* you, brethren, do not grow weary *in* doing good. ¹⁴And if anyone does not obey our word in this epistle, note that person and do not keep company with him, that he may be ashamed. [15]Yet do not count *him* as an enemy, but admonish *him* as a brother.[16]Now may the Lord of peace Himself give you peace always in every way. The Lord *be* with you all.[17]The salutation of Paul with my own hand, which is a sign in every epistle; so I write.[18]The grace of our Lord Jesus Christ *be* with you all. Amen.

The Apostle Paul's teaching is direct and focused to the very end. This time he is dealing with the simple aspect of leadership of hard work. **A leader should work hard and only associate him/herself with others who work hard.**

The essence of leadership is the purposefulness of the leader. This is accomplished through the spirit and attitude of hard work. It is also greatly enhanced—or greatly distracted—by those a hard worker associates. If a hard worker associates with other hard workers—the result will be a powerful and purposeful direction. If an otherwise hard-working leader associates him/herself with slackers—laziness and misdirection will inevitably result.

Hard work is not defined—nor is its meaning—24 hours day/7 day week exhaustion where you don't have a family life or personal time. Instead, hard work is simply the attitude of application a leader either has or hasn't focused in on.

The idea of hard work is a positive one. It is an attitude more than anything else. Let the following attitudes concerning Biblical hard work be part of your life.

> # Attitude:
> # I will watch what people do—not what they say—until I am sure the two things match up.
> # V. 1-3

What people do and what they say are often two different things. We can't control what people do or say but we can observe the difference between them. What someone does speak much louder than what they say. When you see the two things match up, you will know they are a hard worker too.

> # Attitude:
> # I will let God protect me. I will seek God regarding my associations.
> # v. 4

> **Attitude:**
> **I will seek God for**
> **direction and for the**
> **direction of others.**
> **V. 5**

There is no need to stress out over God's direction concerning your associations. Turn the matter over to Him and apply this instruction from the Apostle Paul.

> **Attitude:**
> **There are some people I**
> **just need to avoid.**
> **V. 6-9**

There are some people you can't work with—and others you shouldn't work with. Period—don't beat yourself up over this fact.

This isn't a "cut and dried" thing. Some people work better with others—however—everyone can work with someone. It is not like we dismiss everyone altogether.

140

Attitude:
I won't be nosey because it often interferes with what God is doing.
v. 10-12

Nosiness can really mess things up sometimes. The phrase "on a need to know basis" was created for a reason. (So that those who don't need to know something won't mess up the whole situation for those who do need to know).

Letting God work in a situation requires us to keep our mouths shut, opinions to ourselves, and minding our own business.

Attitude:
I will find what I agree on with others (and agree on that).
V. 13-15

The most effective way to lead is to agree on what you agree on—and camp out on that. Don't fall into the idea "we agree to disagree" or you will spend most of your time reminding each other what it is you disagree on.

This concept works in any relationship or situation.

Whether at work or at home—building a relationship with a colleague or your neighbor—establish the relationship based upon what you agree on and let things grow from there.

****

Effective leadership is a life long journey. We are fortunate to have the Apostle Paul as our mentor all along the way. The Bible has a way of guiding us through all our situations in life.

Leadership is not about personality types—it is about being the person God is developing within you to be. There is always something to learn.

There is nothing a person does that does not require leadership. We are always leading—people need to be equipped to lead.

The most effective leader is the one who was a good follower. Every leader is in the position to follow at some level in their life.

EFFECTIVELY LEAD AND FAITHFULLY FOLLOW!

QUESTIONS FOR DISCUSSION

Explain the idea of hard work as it relates to leadership and the attitudes we should have in relationship to those we associate with:

_____

_____

_____

_____

_____

_____

_____

_____

_____

_____

_____

_____

_____

_____

_____

_____

_____

Being an effective leader requires you to first be a faithful what?

_____

_____

_____

_____

_____

_____

_____